This book belongs to

• •

Draw a picture
of yourself.

COLOR IN

THE DINOSAURS.

Doodlepedia
DINOSAURS

The FUN and CRAZY world of DINOSAURS, DOODLING FUN, and ROARING FACTS

LONDON, NEW YORK, MELBOURNE, MUNICH, AND DELHI

Editor James Mitchem
Senior Designer Sadie Thomas
Designer Ria Holland
Text by James Mitchem
Consultant Darren Naish
US Editor Margaret Parrish
Illustrators Emma Atkinson, Carolyn Bayley,
Holly Blackman, Helen Dodsworth, Chris Howker,
Barney Ibbotson, Evan Nave, Peter Todd,
Dan Woodger, Jay Wright, Jake McDonald
Jacket Designer Jess Bentall
Managing Editor Penny Smith
Managing Art Editor Marianne Markham
Art Director Jane Bull
Category Publisher Mary Ling
Producer, Pre-Production Andy Hilliard
Senior Producer Seyhan Esen
Creative Technical Support Sonia Charbonnier

First American Edition, 2013
Published in the United States in 2013 by
DK Publishing
375 Hudson Street, New York, New York 10014

Copyright© 2013 Dorling Kindersley Limited
187178—08/13
13 14 15 16 17 10 9 8 7 6 5 4 3 2 1
All rights reserved.

A catalog record for this book is available from the
Library of Congress.
ISBN: 978-1-4654-0913-3
Printed and bound in China by Leo Paper Products Ltd.

Discover more at www.dk.com

DRAW THE POOR DINOSAUR A SAFE
ROUTE OUT OF THE MAZE.

FIND AND **COLOR** THE DIFFERENT
TYPES OF SAUROPOD.

Doodlepedia
DINOSAURS

The FUN and CRAZY world of DINOSAURS, DOODLING FUN, and ROARING FACTS

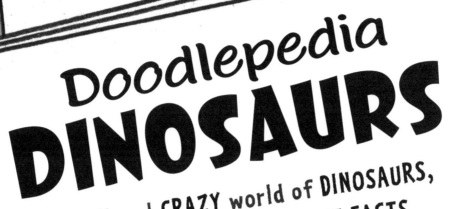

DISCOVER THE DIFFERENT PERIODS OF THE DINOSAUR AGE.

LEARN WHY THE DINOSAURS BECAME EXTINCT.

DOODLE MORE DINOS IN THE EMPTY BOX.

DOODLEPEDIA is exactly what it says on the cover—a book of doodling!

Color, design, and draw all over the pages and learn as you create. Find out about dinosaurs, pterosaurs, marine reptiles, and lots more! Are you ready for oodles of doodling fun? Then turn the page and begin!

Megatooth

If you thought plesiosaurs were scary, you're in for a shock. Megatooth (**MEG-a-tooth**), an ancestor of the great white shark, may have existed 40 million years after the time of the dinosaurs, pterosaurs, and marine reptiles, but it was the all-time **ultimate monster of the deep**. It grew to 65 ft (20 m) long, weighed up to 110 tons (100 metric tons), and is probably the most ferocious predator ever.

Ahh! I'm getting out of here!

START

FINISH

DRAW A WAY OUT OF THE MEGATOOTH MAZE.

DRAW A PATH OUT OF THE MEGATOOTH MAZE.

Crests and plumes

Many dinosaurs had impressive crests and plumes on their heads to **attract mates** and to **threaten rivals**. They came in all shapes and sizes. Can you picture how they might have looked?

PARASAUROLOPHUS

CRYOLOPHOSAURUS

GUANLONG

DRAW CRESTS AND PLUMES ON THE DINOSAURS, THEN MAKE UP YOUR OWN AND...

FINISH THE DINOSAUR'S CRESTS.

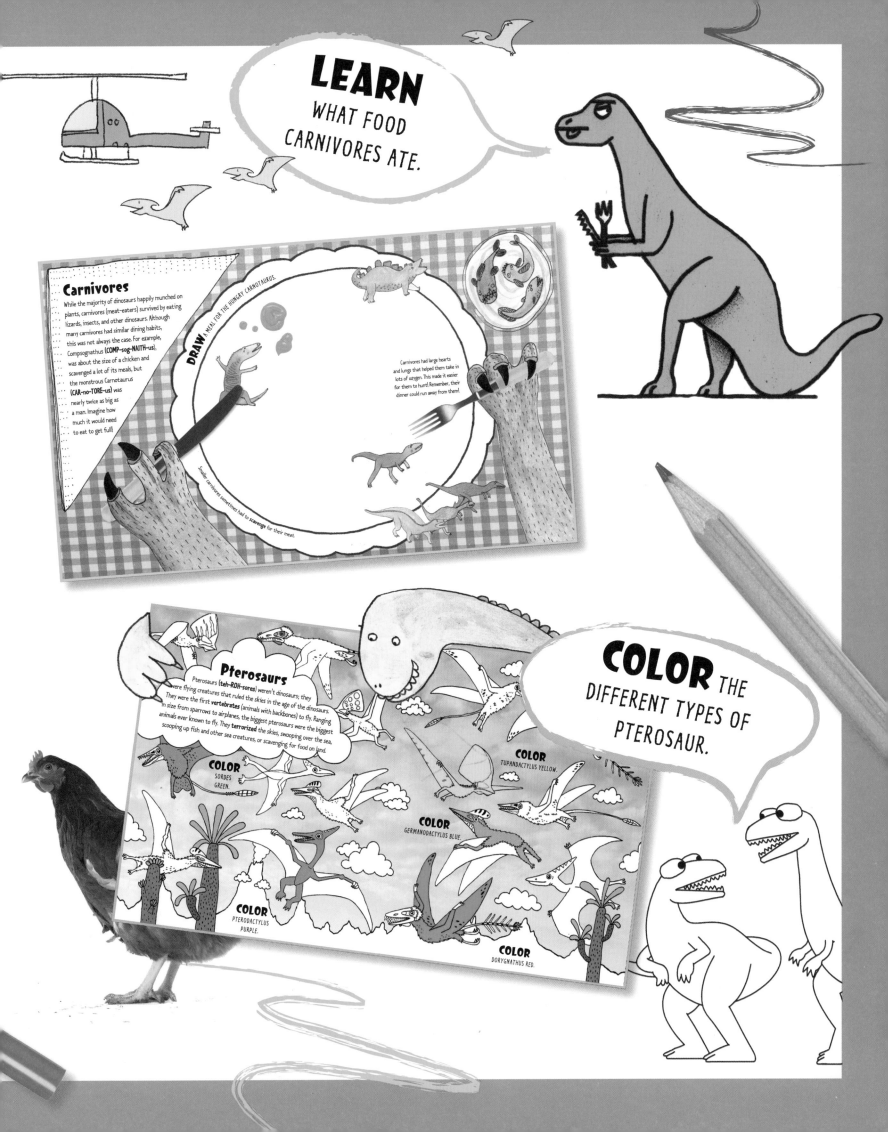

LEARN
WHAT FOOD CARNIVORES ATE.

Carnivores

While the majority of dinosaurs happily munched on plants, carnivores (meat-eaters) survived by eating lizards, insects, and other dinosaurs. Although many carnivores had similar dining habits, this was not always the case. For example, Compsognathus (COMP-sog-NAITH-us), was about the size of a chicken and scavenged a lot of its meals, but the monstrous Carnotaurus (CAR-no-TORE-us) was nearly twice as big as a man. Imagine how much it would need to eat to get full!

DRAW A MEAL FOR THE HUNGRY CARNOTAURUS.

Carnivores had large hearts and lungs that helped them take in lots of oxygen. This made it easier for them to hunt! Remember, their dinner could run away from them!

Smaller carnivores sometimes had to **scavenge** for their meat.

Pterosaurs

Pterosaurs (teh-ROH-sores) weren't dinosaurs; they were flying creatures that ruled the skies in the age of the dinosaurs. They were the first **vertebrates** (animals with backbones) to fly. Ranging in size from sparrows to airplanes, the biggest pterosaurs were the biggest animals ever known to fly. They **terrorized** the skies, swooping over the sea, scooping up fish and other sea creatures, or scavenging for food on land.

COLOR THE DIFFERENT TYPES OF PTEROSAUR.

COLOR SORDES GREEN.

COLOR TUPANDACTYLUS YELLOW.

COLOR GERMANODACTYLUS BLUE.

COLOR PTERODACTYLUS PURPLE.

COLOR DORYGNATHUS RED.

What is a dinosaur?

Long before humans existed, dinosaurs ruled the Earth. For millions of years, these amazing reptiles thrived. Dinosaurs came in all shapes and sizes, and there's still so much we don't know about them. In fact, it's very likely there are new and interesting species we have yet to discover. One thing is for certain though—they were all amazing!

DESIGN
YOUR OWN DINOSAURS.

Dinosaurs can be split into two categories: **ornithischians** (bird-hipped), and **saurischians** (lizard-hipped).

They all had **scaly skin,** but some of them also had **feathers.**

Most dinosaurs ate plants, but many were **meat-eaters**

Many dinosaurs were huge, but others were small.

Some walked on **two legs**, others walked on **four**.

All dinosaurs had **tails.**

All dinosaurs had **clawed or hooved** hands and feet.

The Mesozoic World

If you traveled back in time to see the rise of the dinosaurs, you'd need to go back about 250 million years to a period of the Earth's history called the **Mesozoic Era**. Back then, the Earth was **very different**, and all of the continents were joined together in one big supercontinent called **Pangaea**, which means "All Earth." The Mesozoic Era was divided into three periods: the Triassic, the Jurassic, and the Cretaceous. Each of these periods had its own climate and wildlife.

Because the Mesozoic era was so long, dinosaurs from different periods would have **never met**. In fact, more time separates Stegosaurus from T. rex, than T. rex from us!

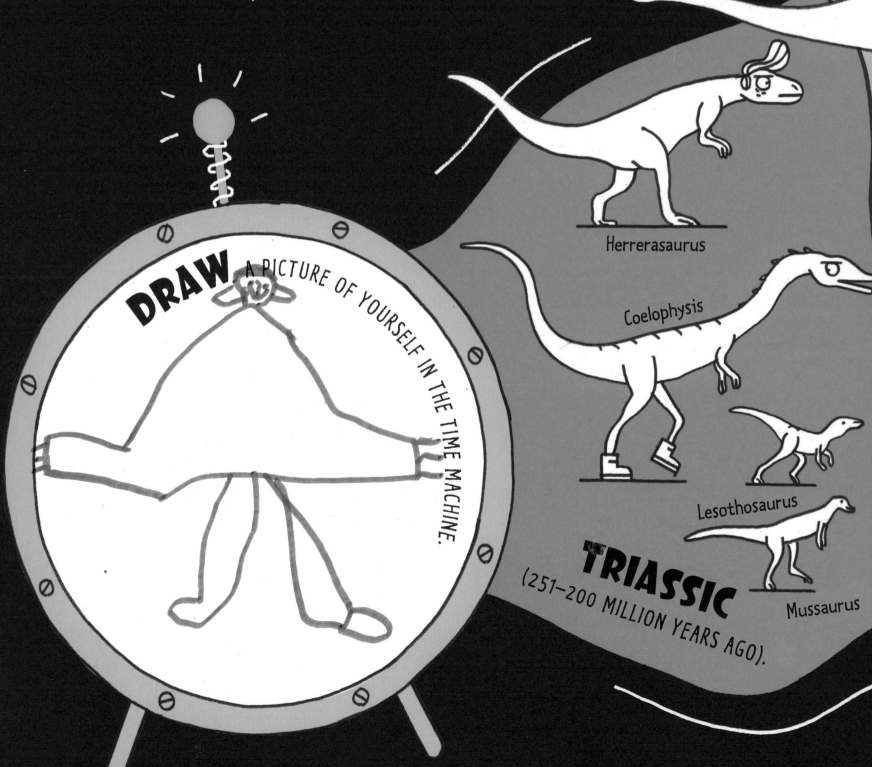

DRAW A PICTURE OF YOURSELF IN THE TIME MACHINE.

Herrerasaurus

Coelophysis

Lesothosaurus

Mussaurus

TRIASSIC
(251–200 MILLION YEARS AGO).

The Earth was very **dry** during the Triassic period. Only the coasts and valleys saw much water.

FINISH THE REST OF THE TRIASSIC SCENE.

Herrerasaurus

Eoraptor

GRRR

We don't have any photos to show us what life was like back then. Everything we know we learn from **studying the remains** of prehistoric things (fossils).

Plateosaurus

The Triassic period

The Earth's scenery was very different during the **Triassic period** (between 251–200 million years ago). It was very hot and the land was covered in large patches of desert, with no grass or flowers and only a few plants. It was during the early Triassic period that the first dinosaurs, such as the Eoraptor **(EE-oh-rap-tor)**, Plateosaurus **(PLATE-ee-oh-SORE-us)**, and Herrerasaurus **(her-RARE-uh-SORE-us)** first emerged.

The Jurassic period

By the time the Triassic period ended 200 million years ago, the Earth had **changed dramatically**. The supercontinent Pangaea **split apart**, creating new continents, oceans, and seas. This made the planet's temperature cool, causing **deserts to shrink and lush forests to grow**. These changes created a lot more food for wildlife. As a result, the Jurassic period saw many **new species** of dinosaur appear.

COLOR IN THE DINOSAURS.

It was during the Jurassic period that the stout Stegosaurus (STEG-oh-SORE-uss), the fierce Allosaurus (al-oh-SORE-us), and the supersized Brachiosaurus (brackee-oh-SORE-uss) existed.

The Cretaceous period

The longest period of the Mesozoic Era was the Cretaceous, which spanned from 145–65 million years ago. It was a time of **incredible diversity**, when many new species of dinosaur appeared. One reason for this was that the continents that formed when Pangaea split drifted farther apart, **spreading dinosaurs to new corners of the Earth.** At the time, the continents were still different from the way they are today, but they were starting to look more like they do now.

PRESENT DAY

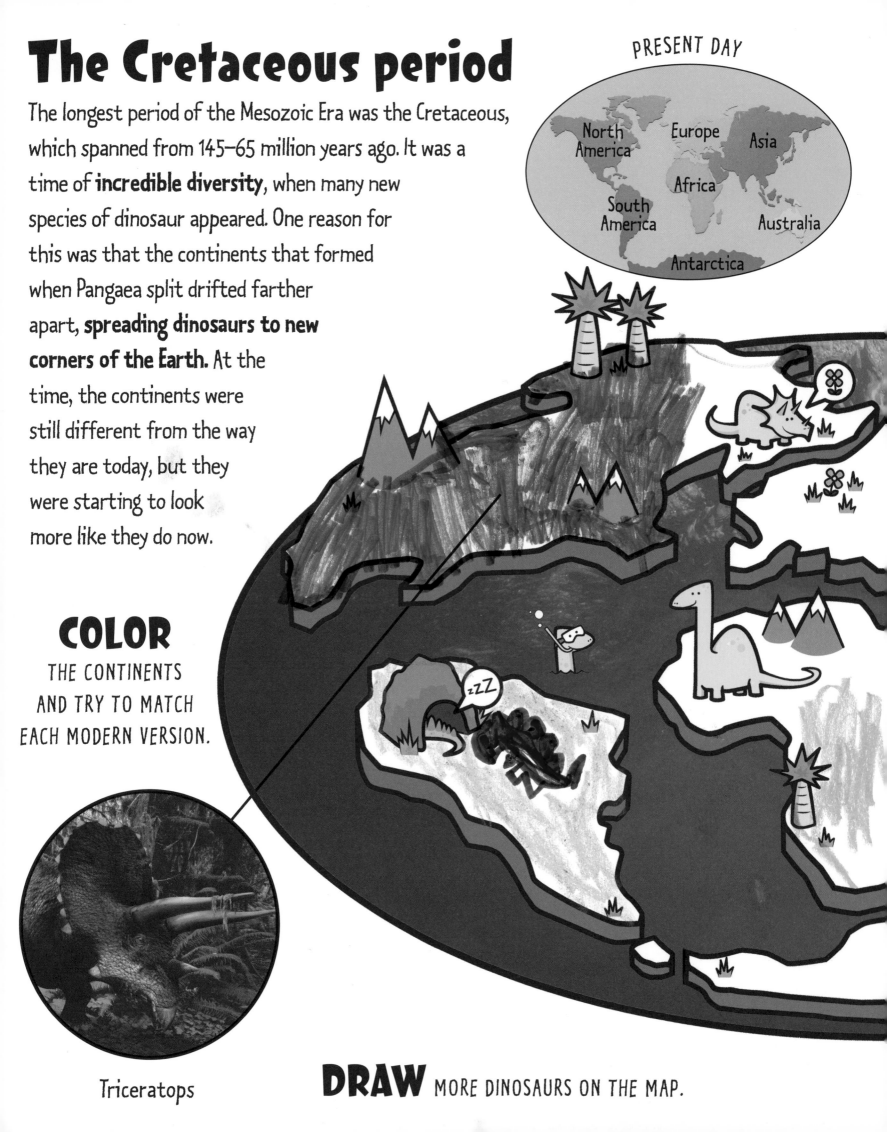

North America

Europe

Asia

Africa

South America

Australia

Antarctica

COLOR

THE CONTINENTS AND TRY TO MATCH EACH MODERN VERSION.

Triceratops

DRAW MORE DINOSAURS ON THE MAP.

The Cretaceous period was when some of the most well-known dinosaurs lived, including Tyrannosaurus rex, Triceratops, and Velociraptor.

The Earth's continents are still moving today, just very slowly!

Tyrannosaurus rex

Herbivores

The biggest dinosaurs of all, sauropods ate only plants. They had to graze **all day** to get enough fuel. It's amazing there was enough food to go around!

The word dinosaur means "terrible lizard," but that doesn't mean they were all terrible! It's true that many dinosaurs were predators, but most were actually **plant-eaters** (herbivores). By the time the Jurassic period rolled around, the Earth was covered with forests—or to a herbivore, **free dinner** for the taking! They just had to get there before all the other dinosaurs showed up!

DRAW MORE DINOSAURS GETTING THEIR DINNER.

CYCADS

BABY
GINGKOS

FERNS

DRAW FOOD IN THE DINOSAURS' GROCERY CARTS BEFORE IT'S ALL GONE!

Carnivores

While the majority of dinosaurs happily munched on plants, carnivores (meat-eaters) survived by eating lizards, insects, and other dinosaurs. Although many carnivores had similar dining habits, this was not always the case. For example, Compsognathus **(COMP-sog-NAITH-us)**, was about the size of a chicken and scavenged a lot of its meals, but the monstrous Carnotaurus **(CAR-no-TORE-us)** was nearly twice as big as a man. Imagine how much it would need to eat to get full!

DRAW A MEAL FOR THE HUNGRY CARNOTAURUS.

Smaller carnivores sometimes had to **scavenge** for their meat.

Carnivores had large hearts and lungs that helped them take in lots of oxygen. This made it easier for them to hunt! Remember, their dinner could run away from them!

SAVE THE TENONTOSAURUS. **DRAW** A SAFE ROUTE OUT OF THE FOREST.

START

Pack attack

Not all predators were big. Sometimes they were **smaller than their prey!** (Imagine your dinner being bigger than you!) To turn the tables, dinosaurs such as Deinonychus (**dye-NON-ee-cuss**) would hunt together, finding prey that had been separated from its **herd** and ganging up on it before moving in for the kill.

FINISH

Deinonychus and Velociraptor were among the deadliest pack hunters.

COLOR

THE FOREST AND CAMOUFLAGE THE SCUTELLOSAURUS.

Habitats

The world of the dinosaurs was very different from ours. Dinosaurs lived in all kinds of **environments** and were always looking for the right place to call **home**.

COLOR THE DESERT.

Deserts—the Earth's climate was **warmer** than it is today, and large areas of desert were found throughout the Mesozoic era.

DRAW MORE DINOSAURS OCCUPYING THE SCRUBLAND.

Too steep!

FINISH THE REST OF THE MOUNTAIN RANGE.

Scrubland—This **semidesert** supported plants that didn't require much water to survive and was home for many early species of dinosaur.

Mountains—These appeared at a growing rate as the Earth's **plates shifted** over the years, but it's likely there wasn't a great deal of food there.

Swampland—Swamps were very common throughout the Cretaceous period and were home to **hadrosaurs** and many other herbivores.

Riverbanks—All living things need water to survive, so a lot of dinosaurs settled close to **riverbanks** and **coasts**.

Forests—Even though dense forests would have helped predators to blend in, they were a **rich source of food** for herbivores such as Triceratops (**try-SERRA-tops**).

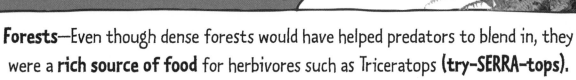

Therizinosaurus

ROLL UP
ROLL UP

Small head

Lethal claws

Feathers

Potbelly

It's easy to see why Therizinosaurus was nicknamed "scythe lizard." Its monstrous claws were almost 3 ft (1 m) long.

Stumpy feet

The strangest dinosaur had to be Therizinosaurus (THERRY-zin-oh-SORE-us). When scientists studied its fossils, they couldn't believe how unusual it was. These dinosaurs stood on their back legs like most predators, but only ate plants. They had lethal claws, but didn't use them for hunting. They had small heads, feathers, stumpy feet, and their large digestive systems gave them big **potbellies!** How weird!

DRAW AND NAME AN EVEN WEIRDER DINOSAUR OF YOUR OWN!

Crests and plumes

Many dinosaurs had impressive crests and plumes on their heads to **attract mates** and to **threaten rivals**. They came in all shapes and sizes. Can you picture how they might have looked?

PARASAUROLOPHUS

Guanlong **(GWON-long)**, an early relative of Tyrannosaurus rex, was discovered in China in 2006.

GUANLONG

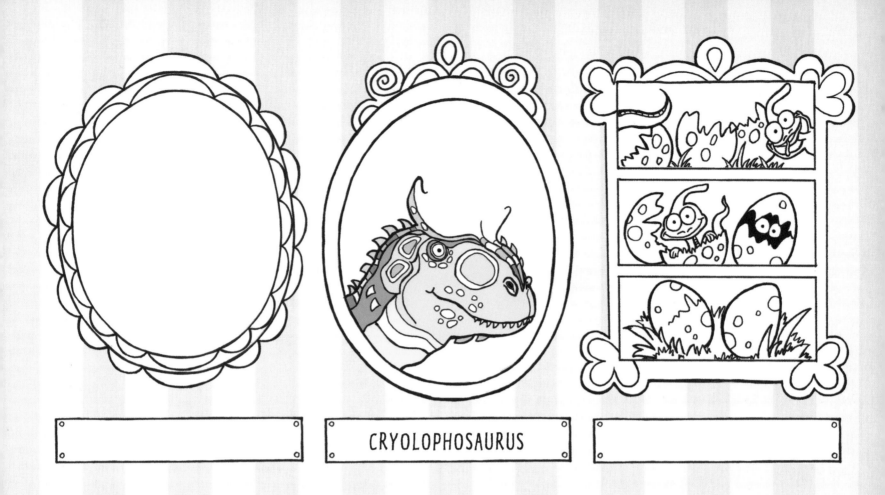

CRYOLOPHOSAURUS

DRAW CRESTS AND PLUMES ON THE DINOSAURS, THEN MAKE UP YOUR OWN AND GIVE THEM NAMES.

Sticking together

For herbivores, danger lurked around every corner. Plant-eaters such as Tenontosaurus (ten-NON-toe-SORE-us) that weren't able to defend themselves looked for **safety in numbers**. They traveled in herds to make sneaky predators think twice about attacking them.

Modern animals such as zebras and wildebeests travel in herds for the same reason.

FINISH THE REST OF THE TENONTOSAURUS HERD.

Bone dome

Pachycephalosaurus (PACK-ee-sef-ah-low-SORE-us) was famous for a very unusual feature. They had a huge, thick skull shaped a little like a **bowling ball**, which might look ugly, but don't tell them that! Experts believe this strange dome was used like a **battering ram** to discourage predators and to intimidate rivals, similar to how stags butt heads today. It's also possible, however, that it was just for show.

The dome was made of **solid bone** and was 10 in (25 cm) thick!

The word pachycephalosaur means "thick-headed lizard."

Walking weapons

Danger was everywhere during the time of the dinosaurs—even predators were sometimes **prey for bigger dinosaurs themselves!** Only the biggest and strongest such as Tyrannosaurus rex could feel safe at all times. The scariest predators didn't need any special weapons to take down their prey—they had their own!

T. rex's jaw was so powerful that it could **crush the bones** of its prey with ease.

Allosaurus had a weak jaw, but very sharp teeth. It's possible it **slashed** its prey rather than try to bite it.

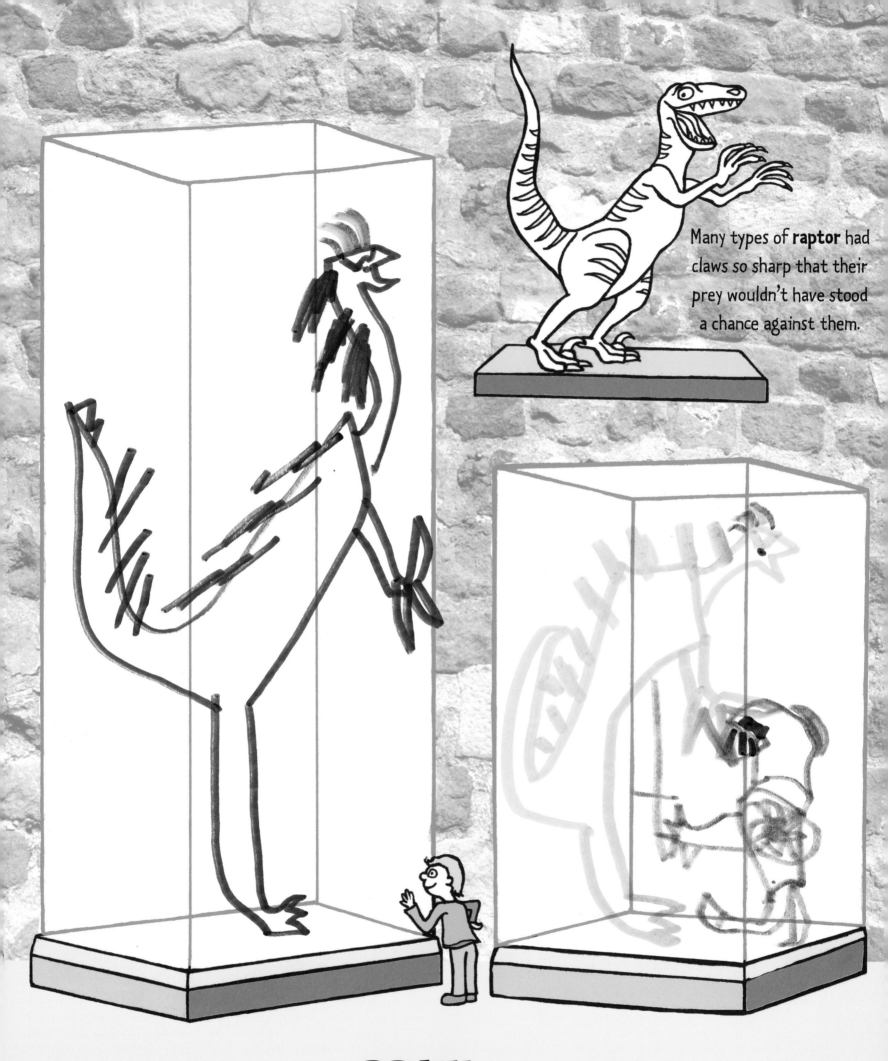

Many types of **raptor** had claws so sharp that their prey wouldn't have stood a chance against them.

DRAW YOUR OWN DINOSAURS WITH DEADLY WEAPONS.

Defense

No dinosaur wanted to be an easy meal. Some would try to fight off predators with their claws and teeth, but others—such as a group of dinosaur called **ankylosaurs**—had special defensive features such as plates and spines. One of these was Euoplocephalus (**YOU-owe-plo-SEFF-ah-luss**), which was **built like a tank** and had a crushing club made of bone at the end of its tail that it would swing at attacking predators.

Euoplocephalus was so armored with spikes and plates that even its **eyelids** were protected!

DESIGN YOUR OWN ARMORED DINOSAUR.

FIGHTING BACK

When under attack from predators, dinosaurs were faced with a choice: to either **run or fight.** And sometimes the best defense was a good offense. Several herbivores had more than just armor and were equipped with deadly weapons of their own to help them **fight back** against their enemies.

STEGOSAURUS

Stegosaurus had **razor-sharp** spikes on its tail, which it could whip at enemies.

PENTACERATOPS

Pentaceratops and other ceratopsians could use their large **horns** as weapons of defense.

IGUANODON

Iguanodon had sharp **spikes** on its hands to jab at attackers.

DIPLODOCUS

Not only was Diplodocus huge, but it could also use its long tail like a **whip.**

DRAW THE FIGHTING DINOSAURS.

FINISH
DRAWING THE SPINES ON THE DINOSAURS.

OURANOSAURUS

Spines and sails

It wasn't just their teeth and claws that helped dinosaurs stand out. Several dinosaurs had sail-like spines on their backs and necks. While these would have mainly been used to **attract mates** and **scare off rivals**, experts believe that they might also have helped dinosaurs manage their body temperature.

RAYOSOSAURUS

SPINOSAURUS

One of the most impressive spines belonged to **Spinosaurus,** the largest predator ever to walk the Earth. It was **even bigger** than Tyrannosaurus rex!

Mini monster

Who says you had to be big to be a predator? Compsognathus **(COMP-sog-NAITH-us)**, a predator from the Jurassic period, was no bigger than a **chicken**! It used its speed and agility to chase down fast-moving lizards and insects, scavenge other predators' kills, and even sometimes **gang up on** and take down larger prey.

It may have been small, but it was fast. Despite its size, Compsognathus could **run at speeds of more than 25 mph** (40 kph).

25

DRAW

THE REST OF THE
COMPSOGNATHUS PACK.

Compsognathus may have
been covered in **feathers,
fuzz,** or **scales** to help
it stay warm.

Grazing giants

The Jurassic period saw the rise of the sauropods—the largest creatures ever to walk the Earth. The largest of these, Argentinosaurus **(ARE-jen-teen-oh-SORE-us)**, grew to 120 ft (36 m) long and weighed as much as **13 elephants**. It would have needed to eat all day to have enough energy to move!

A single Brachiosaurus would have had to eat around 400 lb (180 kg) of food **every day!**

COLOR
ARGENTINOSAURUS
GREEN.

COLOR
DIPLODOCUS RED.

Sauropods had long necks so they could reach food other dinosaurs couldn't. Some could even stand on their **hind legs**!

Sauropods were plant-eaters, but that doesn't mean they couldn't defend themselves from predators. They were so massive that they could **crush** any attackers.

COLOR
BRACHIOSAURUS YELLOW.

COLOR
SALTASAURUS BLUE.

Titans of the Earth

Tyrannosaurus rex gets all the glory, but plenty of other giant predators existed. In fact, T. rex's "cousin" Giganotosaurus (**gig-AN-oh-toe-SORE-rus**) was just as big. It's lucky they lived 10 million years apart or there would have been **nasty fights** at mealtimes!

Experts believe that Giganotosaurus had a brain the shape of a **banana!**

No complete Giganotosaurus skeleton has been found, but experts believe these giants were about 45 ft (13.5 m) long and weighed as much as **125 people!**

COLOR GIGANOTOSAURUS BLUE.

COLOR CARNOTAURUS RED.

COLOR
TYRANNOSAURUS GREEN.

COLOR
TYRANNOTITAN YELLOW.

COLOR
CARCHARODONTOSAURUS PURPLE.

DRAW MORE PARVICURSORS.

Little and large

Dinosaurs came in all shapes and sizes, and while we usually think of them

as colossal **giants** roaming the land, a few of them were actually tiny.

For example, while the gigantic Brachiosaurus **(brack–ee–oh–SORE–us)**,

a sauropod from the Jurassic, grew to 82 ft (25 m) long from head

to tail, the tiny Parvicursor **(PAR–vee–cur–SORE)**, from the

Late Cretaceous, was just 18 in (45 cm) from end to end!

Brachiosaurus may have
been big, but it didn't have
a lot going on upstairs—its
brain was about the
size of a **grapefruit!**

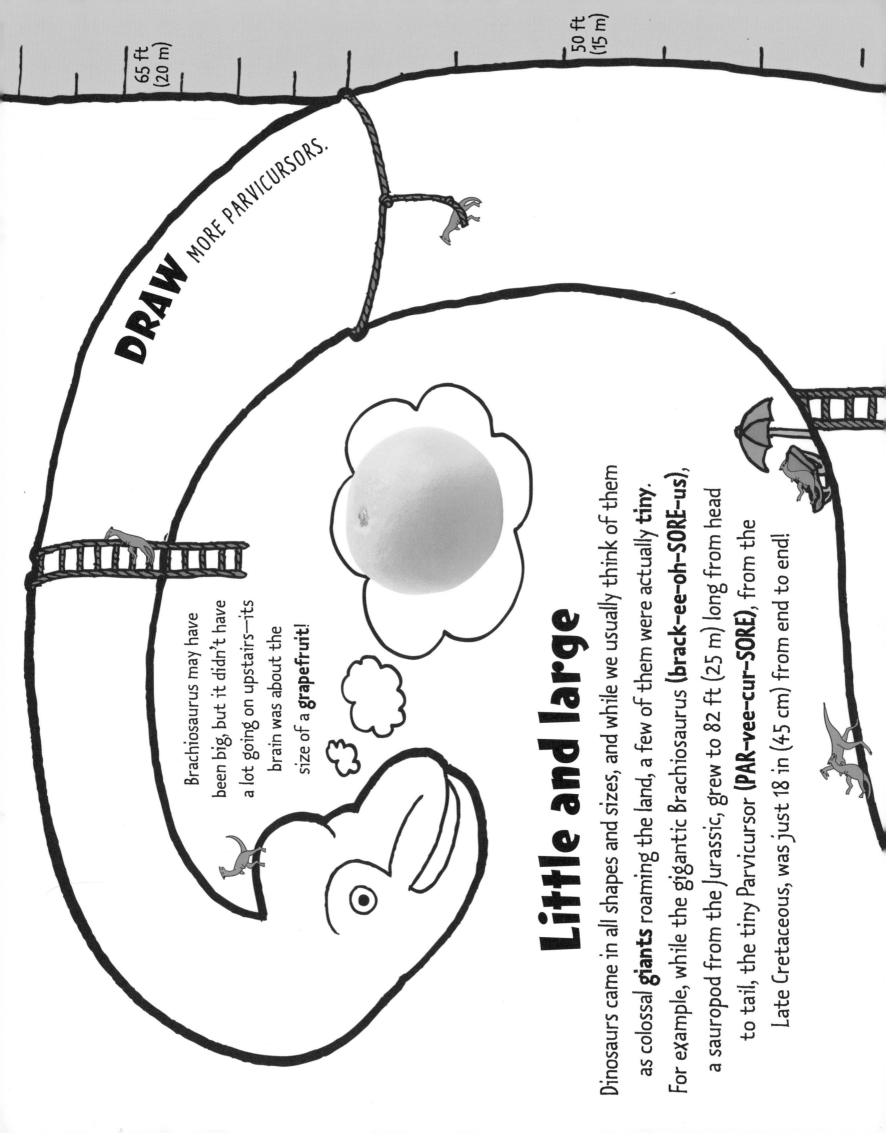

33 ft
(10 m)

16 ft
(5 m)

Parvicursors had fairly large claws on their hands, but these were probably used for **digging** rather than for defense.

Fast and slow

Fossils give us clues about how fast dinosaurs could run. Speed varied between species, and while no dinosaur could sprint like the fastest modern land animal, the **cheetah**, which can run at **70 mph** (114 kph), smaller dinosaurs were probably very fast. Others, such as the giant sauropods, were slow pokes.

Brachiosaurus weighed so much that it likely couldn't move faster than 3.5 mph (6 kph)!

Ankylosaurus was built like a tank and **didn't need to** run away from predators, so it was probably slow-moving.

Ankylosaurus

Brachiosaurus

DRAW MORE RACING DINOSAURS.

Predators walked on two legs to be able to move fast enough to catch their food.

Predator and prey

All dinosaurs had to eat to survive, and while herbivores were happy to chomp on plants, carnivores had something a little fresher in mind! Because of this, plant-eaters were always on the lookout for **hungry predators** ready to turn them into their next meal!

CAN YOU TELL THE HUNTERS FROM THE HUNTED?
COLOR THE PREDATORS ORANGE AND THE PREY YELLOW.

Herbivores were slow-moving and walked on four legs.

Stegosaurus

Don't let the fact that Stegosaurus **(STEG-oh-SORE-uss)** was a plant-eater trick you into thinking it was easy prey. Stegosauruses grew to 30 ft (9 m) long and weighed as much as **4.5 tons.** (4 metric tons). With their impressive plates and **sharp, spiked tails**, they were well-equipped to fend off even the fiercest predators of the Jurassic period.

FINISH THE SPIKES ON THE TAIL.

HELP THE STEGOSAURUS FIGHT OFF THE ALLOSAURUS.
DRAW MORE DEFENSIVE PLATES.

Stegosaurus certainly wasn't
the smartest dinosaur in the
herd. Its brain was no bigger
than a **walnut!**

Certain dinosaurs would **sit on their nests** the way that birds do.

START

Baby dinosaurs

Dinosaurs were reptiles, so scientists always thought that they probably laid eggs. But it wasn't until 1920, when the remains of the eggs and nests of a dinosaur called Oviraptor **(oh-vee-RAP-tor)** were found in the **Gobi Desert, China,** that they knew this for certain. This huge discovery helped scientists to understand much more about dinosaur life.

The temperature of dinosaur eggs helped **determine the gender** of the babies. The warmer the eggs, the more likely it was that they would hatch as males.

DRAW THE OVIRAPTOR A SAFE ROUTE BACK TO HER NEST.

FINISH

Oviraptor would sometimes dig its nests in sand or soil.

Parasaurolophus

During the Cretaceous period, a group of dinosaur called hadrosaurs, or "duck-billed" dinosaurs, emerged. Among these was Parasaurolophus (PA-ra-SORE-oh-LOAF-uss), a large plant-eater with hundreds of grinding teeth for mashing up food. They were common and traveled in large herds and are sometimes thought of as the dinosaur version of cows!

Unlike most other herbivores, hadrosaurs could walk on either two or four legs.

Parasaurolophus was **surprisingly big** for prey, and adults could grow to be 33 ft (10 m) long. No wonder it was a favorite meal for many carnivores—it made for very big portions!

CONNECT THE DOTS TO REVEAL THE PICTURE.

No one is certain if dinosaurs **communicated with sound**, but experts believe they probably did. One reason for this is that Parasaurolophus's crest contained a series of tubes that **connected to the nostrils**—which meant it might have worked like a trumpet.

Deinonychus

While teeth were the weapon of choice for many dinosaurs, others inflicted damage with their **claws**. Perhaps the scariest of these dinosaurs was Deinonychus **(dye-NON-ee-cuss)**, a speedy pack hunter from the Early Cretaceous. In addition to the sharp claws on its hands, Deinonychus had a monstrous upturned **sickle claw** on each foot that it used to deliver lethal strikes.

Deinonychus means "terrible claw," and it's easy to see why!

Deinonychus was a fierce hunter, but it was only 10 ft (3 m) long, so it roamed in packs to take down larger prey.

FINISH THE REST OF THE DEINONYCHUS PACK.

The long tail was held stiff to help with balance while running.

Dressed to frill

Known for their **horns** and neck frills, ceratopsians were a group of herbivores from the Cretaceous period. They might look scary, but their large frills and horns were **only for protection**, and their sharp beaks were used to **rip up plants** for food.

Although they look a little similar, ceratopsians are not related to the modern **rhinoceros**.

COLOR PROTOCERATOPS GREEN.

There is lots of fossil evidence to suggest that many **fierce battles** took place between Triceratops and T. rex.

COLOR STYRACOSAURUS PURPLE.

COLOR PENTACERATOPS BLUE.

Pentaceratops had a **giant skull** measuring 10 ft (3 m) long!

COLOR TRICERATOPS RED.

COLOR CHASMOSAURUS YELLOW.

The ultimate predator

Tyrannosaurus rex (**TIE-ran-oh-SORE-us**), or T. rex for short, was a ferocious hunter with a massive skull and **bone-crushing teeth**. At 13 ft (4 m) tall and 40 ft (12 m) long, it weighed as much as **five cars**. It was one of the biggest predators that ever lived, and it terrorized the forests of what is now North America until it became extinct 65 million years ago. Phew!

FINISH THE T. REX'S DINNER INSIDE ITS STOMACH.

Tyrannosaurus means "tyrant lizard" in Greek.

I am the king of the dinosaurs, and I had very **bad breath**! Some experts believe that rotting meat stuck in my teeth could have made my bite **poisonous**, as well as crushing.

DRAW ANOTHER T. REX IN THE BACKGROUND.

Pterosaurs

Pterosaurs (**teh-ROH-sores**) weren't dinosaurs; they were flying creatures that ruled the skies in the age of the dinosaurs. They were the first **vertebrates** (animals with backbones) to fly. Ranging in size from sparrows to airplanes, the biggest pterosaurs were the biggest animals ever known to fly. They **terrorized** the skies, swooping over the sea, scooping up fish and other sea creatures, or scavenging for food on land.

COLOR SORDES GREEN.

COLOR PTERODACTYLUS PURPLE.

COLOR
TUPANDACTYLUS YELLOW.

COLOR
GERMANODACTYLUS BLUE.

COLOR
DORYGNATHUS RED.

Quetzalcoatlus was a **soarer** rather than a flier. It relied on strong winds to travel through the air.

DRAW MORE SOARING QUETZALCOATLUSES.

Quetzalcoatlus

The largest creature ever to fly was the monstrous pterosaur Quetzalcoatlus **(KWETS-ul-coe-AT-luss)**. This giant ruled the Cretaceous skies, casting a wide shadow over the ground wherever it flew. Its **wingspan** was a massive 40 ft (12 m) across, the size of a small plane!

The first bird

Believe it or not, birds are the descendants of dinosaurs. Technically, **they are dinosaurs—** the only surviving group! The earliest known bird is Archaeopteryx **(ar-kee-OP-ter-ix)**, which appeared in the Jurassic period. It had the feathered tail and wings of a bird, but the claws of a dinosaur.

COLOR
IN THE FUNKY FEATHERS.

Archaeopteryx was about the same size as a modern raven.

No one knows what color their feathers were. For all we know they could have been **bright pink or orange!**

COLOR
TYLOSAURUS PURPLE.

COLOR
PLESIOSAURUS BLUE.

Creatures of the deep

Dinosaurs ruled the land, and pterosaurs dominated the sky, but it was **marine reptiles** that **lurked beneath the waves** during the Mesozoic Era. The largest of these massive monsters could grow to 65 ft (20 m) long, and although they spent their lives in the water, they all **breathed air.**

The skull of Deinosuchus (die-no-SUE-kus)— a relative of modern crocodiles—was 6 ft (1.8 m) long, and a full-grown Deinosuchus weighed up to 5.5 tons (5 metric tons)!

COLOR DEINOSUCHUS YELLOW.

COLOR ELASMOSAURUS RED.

Elasmosaurus had **72 bones** in its neck!

COLOR KRONOSAURUS GREEN.

Rhomaleosaurus

The words "sea monsters" come to mind when you think of Rhomaleosaurus **(ROME-alley-oh-SORE-us)**. They grew to up to 21 ft (7 m) long and in many ways were like the aquatic version of Tyrannosaurus rex. They **terrorized** the Jurassic seas, feasting on fish, squid, and smaller marine reptiles.

Rhomaleosaurus glided through the water using its four flippers like wings to **"fly"** underwater. Penguins and sea lions do a similar thing today.

CONNECT THE DOTS TO REVEAL THE PICTURE.

It's thought that like a lot of ocean predators, Rhomaleosaurus had a pale belly and dark back, making it **harder to spot** from both above and below.

Megatooth

If you thought plesiosaurs were scary, you're in for a shock. Megatooth (**MEG-a-tooth**), an ancestor of the great white shark, may have existed 40 million years after the time of the dinosaurs, pterosaurs, and marine reptiles, but it was the all-time **ultimate monster of the deep**. It grew to 65 ft (20 m) long, weighed up to 110 tons (100 metric tons), and is probably the most ferocious predator ever.

START

Megatooth's teeth were the size of dinner plates, and it had about **250** of them. That would mean a lot of toothpaste!

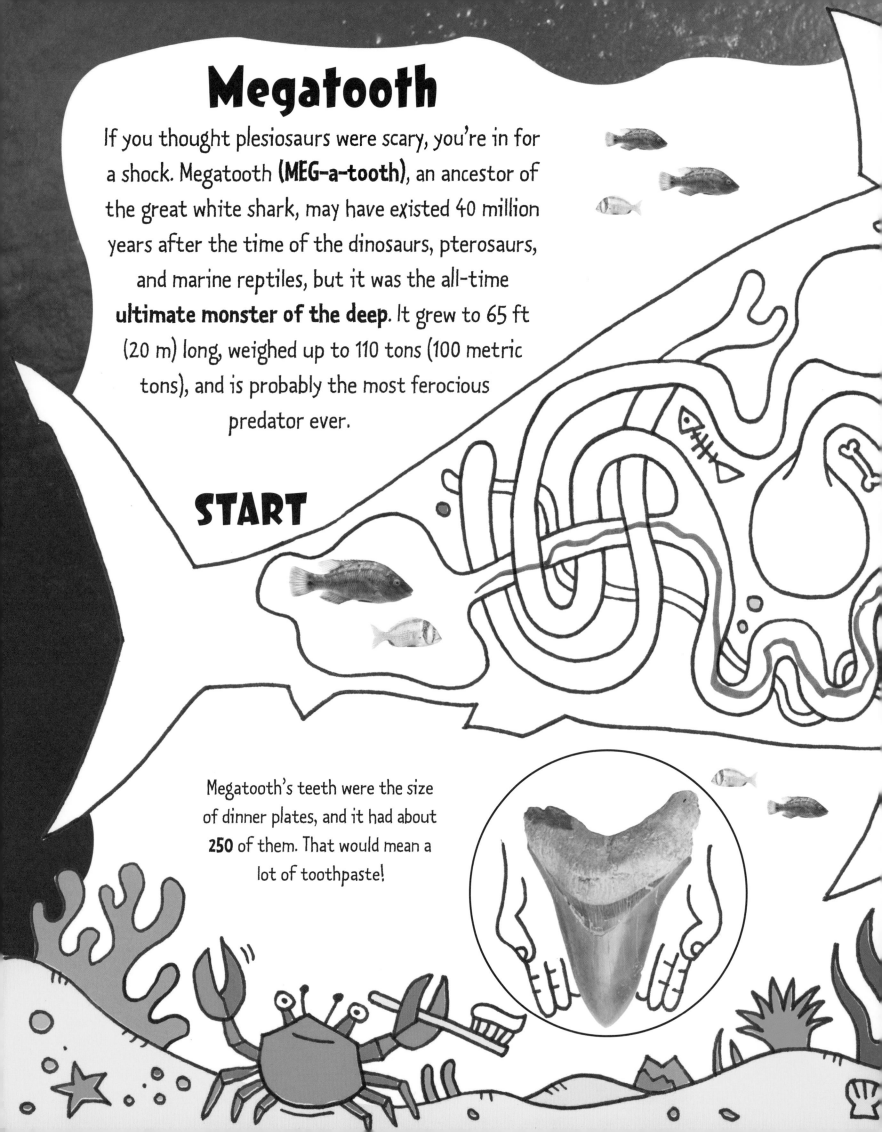

DRAW A WAY OUT OF THE MEGATOOTH MAZE.

Great white shark

The ultimate beast!

All dinosaurs were amazing creatures, but some dinosaurs were a little more spectacular than others. These dinosaurs were among the **fastest, strongest, scariest, and most interesting** to have lived—but can you imagine what a dinosaur with all of these qualities combined would be like?

LONGEST NECK
MAMENCHISAURUS

PERIOD	JURASSIC
SIZE	★★★★★
SPEED	★
INTELLIGENCE	★★

BIGGEST BRAIN
TROODON

PERIOD	CRETACEOUS
SIZE	★
SPEED	★★★★
INTELLIGENCE	★★★★★

STRONGEST BITE
T. REX

PERIOD	CRETACEOUS
SIZE	★★★★
SPEED	★★★
INTELLIGENCE	★

DRAW THE SCARIEST DINOSAURS THAT NEVER LIVED BY COMBINING THE FEATURES OF THE OTHER DINOSAURS.

BEST ARMOR
ANKYLOSAURUS

PERIOD	CRETACEOUS
SIZE	★★★
SPEED	★★
INTELLIGENCE	★★

DEADLIEST CLAWS
UTAHRAPTOR

PERIOD	CRETACEOUS
SIZE	★★★
SPEED	★★★★
INTELLIGENCE	★★★

FASTEST LEGS
STRUTHIOMIMUS

PERIOD	CRETACEOUS
SIZE	★★
SPEED	★★★★★
INTELLIGENCE	★★★★

Where did they go?

At the end of the Cretaceous period, dinosaurs were **thriving** like never before. Then, about 65 million years ago—with the exception of several species of bird—they **mysteriously died out**. The reason why this happened puzzled scientists for years, but they now believe that a **massive meteorite** crashed into the Earth. This caused earthquakes, tsunamis, volcanic eruptions, and threw up a cloud of dust so big that it blocked out the Sun.

The **remains of a crater** 112 miles (180 km) wide can be found in Mexico. Experts believe this is where the meteorite crash-landed.

EEEK

DRAW MORE SCARED DINOSAURS!

Other theories about why the dinosaurs became extinct include an ice age and a dinosaur **plague**.

Scientists estimate that the meteorite would have been roughly 6 miles (10 km) wide and struck the Earth at a **staggering** 60,000 mph (100,000 kph)!

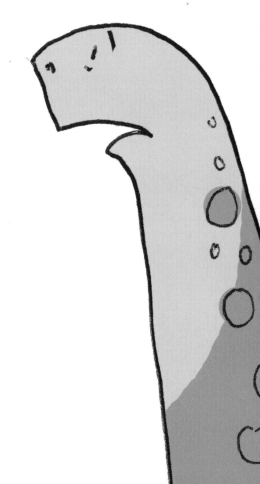

THE DAILY DINO

WHAT SURVIVED?

SEE THE LATEST IN DINOSAUR FASHION!

In the millions of years that followed the destruction of the dinosaurs, many new species of animal **came and went**. However, a handful of creatures, other than birds from the Mesozoic Era, managed to **survive the extinction** and are still around today—on land, in the sea, and in the air.

DRAW THE REST OF THE SURVIVORS.

Various species of **fish, shark, and jellyfish** were among the creatures that survived in the seas.

It was only **small animals** such as lizards, insects, snakes, and crocodiles that survived on land.

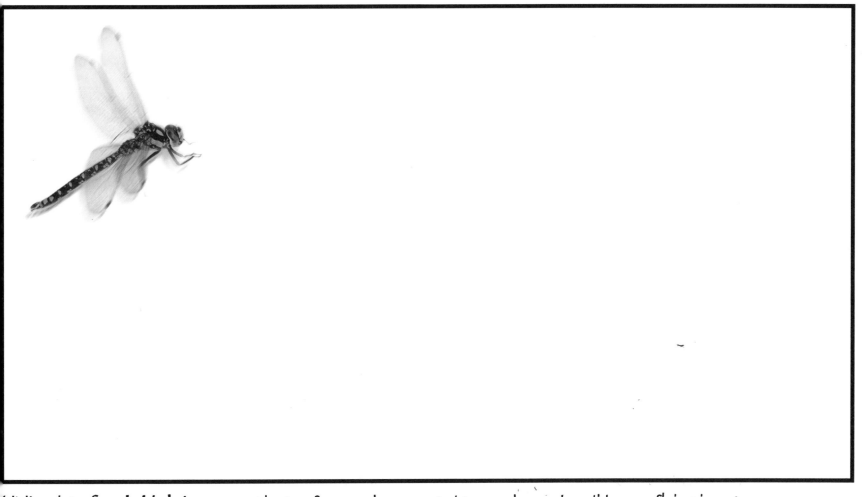

While a lot of **early birds** became extinct, a few species managed to survive, and so did many flying insects.

FINISH

A MODERN CITY WITH PEOPLE AND DINOSAURS LIVING TOGETHER!

What if they weren't extinct?

In the years that followed the extinction caused by the meteorite, the world became a **very different** place. The continents shifted, the climate changed, and thousands of new species of animal and plant evolved. Eventually, human beings emerged and became the Earth's most **dominant species.** But can you imagine what the world would be like if the dinosaurs hadn't become extinct? Would we keep dinosaurs as pets? Or would they be destructive and try to eat us?

Turning to stone

Everything we know about dinosaurs, pterosaurs, and marine reptiles we learned from their **fossilized remains**. Fossils are the stone remnants of things that lived long ago and that have been preserved in the Earth's layers.

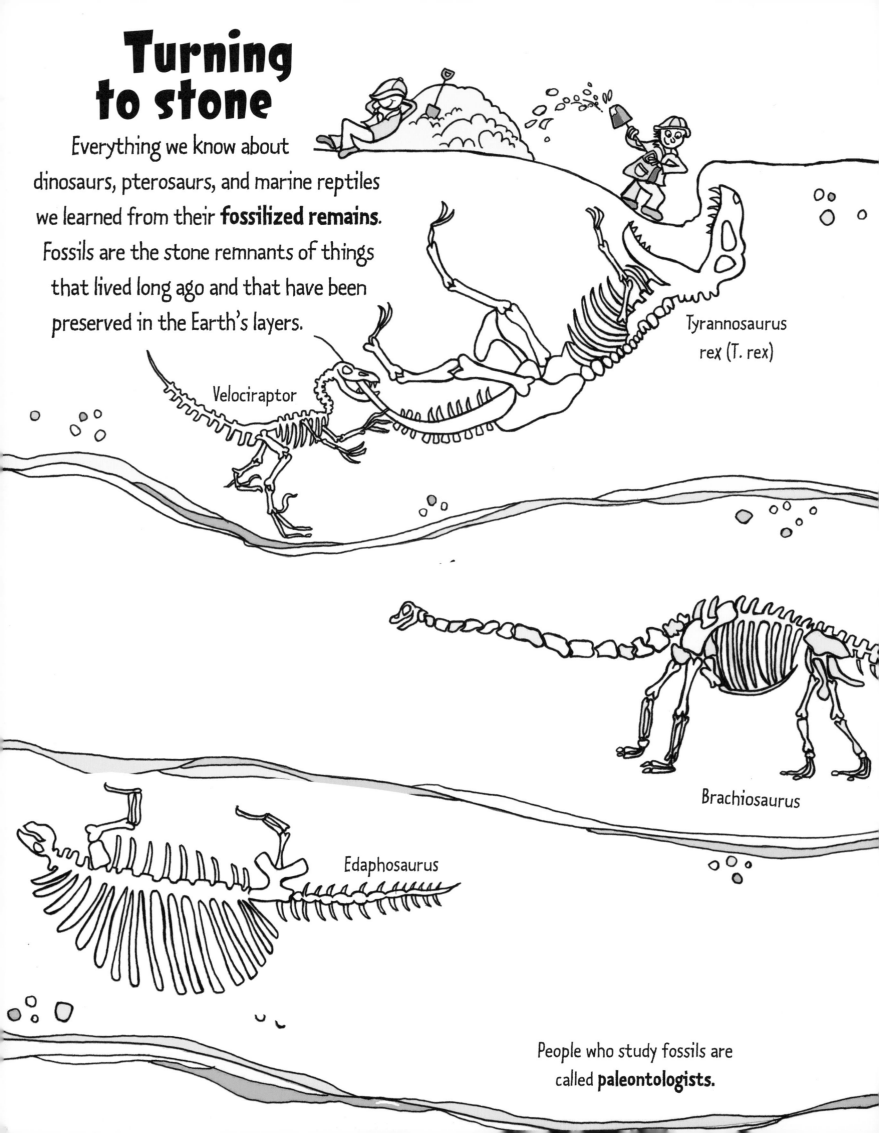

Tyrannosaurus rex (T. rex)

Velociraptor

Brachiosaurus

Edaphosaurus

People who study fossils are called **paleontologists**.

Fossils are rare. Most dinosaurs simply decayed and **disappeared forever**. Only a few of the dinosaurs that lived have been, or will be found, as fossils.

Triceratops

Pterodactylus

DRAW MORE FOSSILS IN THE EARTH.

Fossilized eggs, feathers, footprints, and even **dinosaur poop** have been found. These all help us to understand more about prehistoric life.

Studying fossils

Not only are fossils **rare**, but they're also very fragile, and it takes a lot of hard work and patience for **paleontologists** (fossil experts) to get them out of the ground. When a fossil is discovered, huge dig sites are set up, and it can take months before the fossils are fully excavated for study in a lab.

Fossils are usually encased in rock, so paleontologists need a lot of tools to dig them out without breaking them.

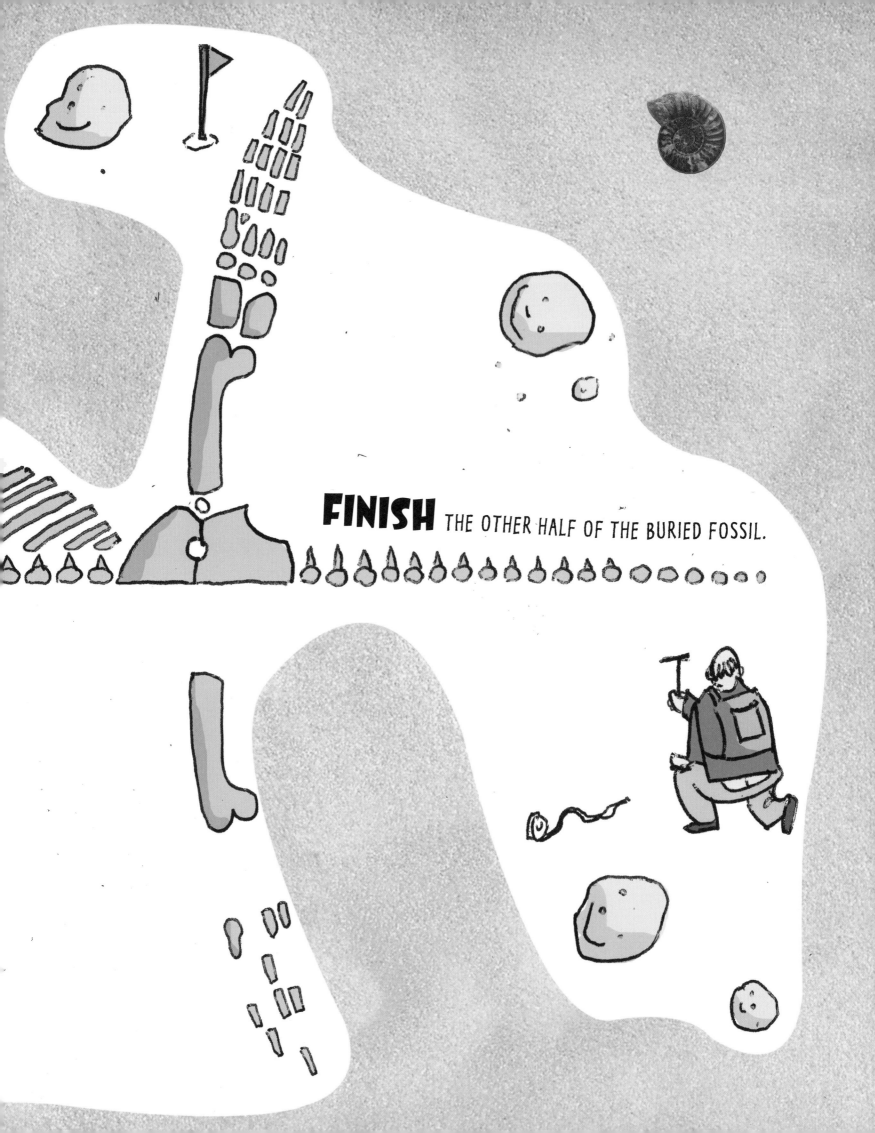

FINISH THE OTHER HALF OF THE BURIED FOSSIL.

Dinosaurs on display

The dinosaurs might not be around anymore, but that shouldn't stop you from seeing what they were like. Museums have incredible dinosaur exhibits on display, including fossils that are **hundreds of millions** of years old, and even full skeletons!

SOME OF THE T. REX BONES HAVE FALLEN OFF! **DRAW** THEM BACK ON TO FINISH THE DISPLAY.

"Sue" the T. rex fossil at the Field Museum, Chicago, is the most complete T. rex fossil in the world. It cost the museum a whopping **$8.4 million** when they bought it in 1997.

TYRANNOSAURUS REX

Draw your own dinosaur

Now that you've learned all about these amazing creatures, draw **one of your own**. Who knows, one day a paleontologist might discover one that looks just like it!

TYRANTOSAURUS

DRAW SOMETHING PREHISTORIC TO COMPLETE THE BOOK.

DK WOULD LIKE TO THANK

The publisher would like to thank the following for their kind permission to reproduce their photographs:

Peter Minister for his Deinonychus image.

All other images © Dorling Kindersley
For further information see: www.dkimages.com